0/01

W9-AQS-266

"WALDO

Festival of Lights

The Story of Hanukkah

Retold by Maida Silverman

Illustrated by Carolyn S. Ewing

ALADDIN PAPERBACKS

Long ago, the Jewish people lived in the kingdom of Judea. Antiochus IV ruled the land. He worshipped Greek gods, but Jews were allowed to worship their God, as they had always done.

Jerusalem was the capital city of Judea and many people lived there. The Holy Temple stood on a high hill in the city. Jews came there to pray to the Lord.

Life was peaceful. Children went to school. Merchants sold their wares. Farmers planted crops. Shepherds tended flocks of sheep and goats.

Antiochus was not happy being King of Judea. He wanted to be King of Egypt, too. He made war on the Egyptians, but was defeated. This put him in a very bad mood. He decided to go to Jerusalem. "There are treasures in the Temple," he said. "I am King. I'll take them for myself!"

The King and his army marched into the Holy Temple. They stole gold cups and dishes used by the High Priest. They took furniture, curtains, and the beautiful Menorah lamp. Soldiers struck down anyone who tried to stop them.

King Antiochus was furious because the Jews fought his soldiers. He had his army burn down their houses and took many Jews away to be slaves.

The King put his soldiers in charge of Jerusalem. They brought statues of Greek gods to the Holy Temple and made offerings to them.

Antiochus thought about how the Jews fought to protect their Temple. "They love their God too much," he said. "They must not pray to him anymore."

Messengers were sent to Judea with the King's orders.

"The Jews may not keep the Sabbath as a day of rest. They may not follow their laws and customs, or study Holy Books. They must worship Greek gods."

The Jews refused to obey the cruel decree. They prayed and studied in secret.

One morning, the King's patrol came to the village of Modin. They set up a statue and altar in the square. Everyone was ordered to go there. A soldier told Mattathias, the village elder, to step forward.

"Bow down to the god and sacrifice this pig to him," he commanded.

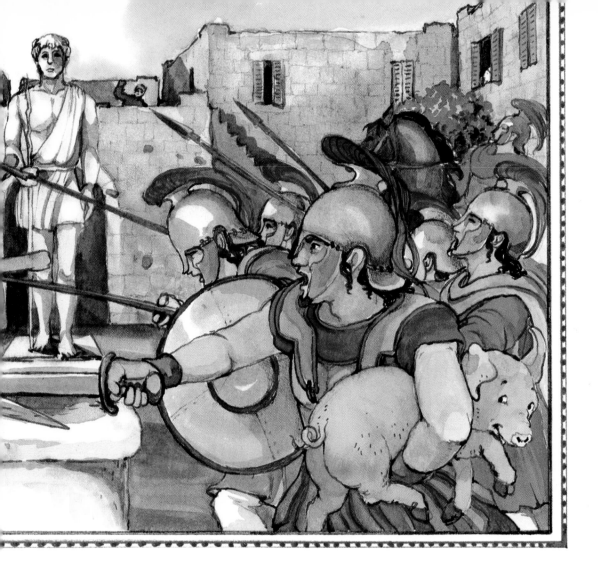

"We serve our Lord, the One God," cried Mattathias. "We will never worship idols!" He turned to his five sons. "Attack the soldiers!" he shouted. The villagers joined Mattathias' sons. They tore down the statue and altar. Taken by surprise, the soldiers fled.

"Today, a few soldiers came," said Mattathias. "Many more will return tomorrow. We must leave Modin. And we must prepare to fight for freedom to worship the Lord."

Everyone hastily packed food and clothing. They took the weapons the soldiers left behind. They followed Mattathias to caves in the mountains.

Mattathias spoke to his son Judah. "You are a Maccabee, which means

hammer. You are brave and strong. Make our people into Maccabees, to strike against the King!"

Judah and his brothers taught the people how to fight. They made surprise attacks and won small battles. Word of the Maccabees spread and many people joined them.

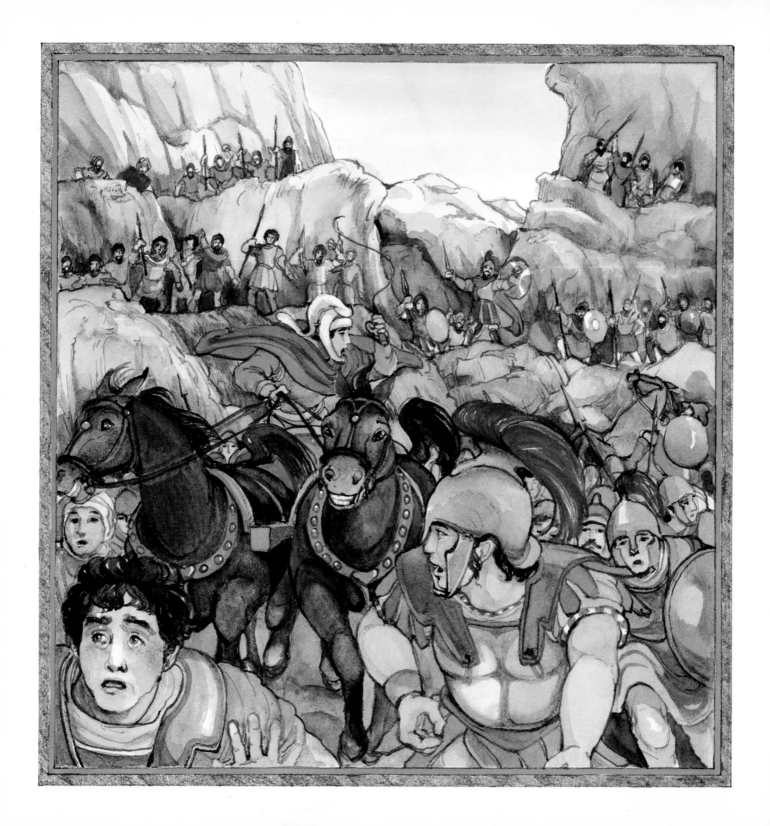

King Antiochus was very angry when he heard about Judah and his men. He sent for Appolonius, his favorite general.

"Take an army to Judea," he said. "Attack the Maccabees and defeat them!"

The General and his soldiers had to march through a narrow mountain pass. Judah and his fighters surprised them there. The Maccabees were out-numbered, but they won the battle. Judah found the General's sword. He kept it and used it for the rest of his life.

The King was furious at the Maccabee victory. He sent for Lysias, his finest general. "Take my fighting elephants and my best soldiers! Crush the Maccabees once and for all!"

Judah and his men watched the huge army camp on the plain. They prayed to God for strength to defeat so strong an enemy.

This was the biggest battle of all. The Maccabees fought so fiercely that Lysias had to order a retreat. All the King's soldiers left the land of Judea.

The Maccabees returned to Jerusalem, and people welcomed them joyfully. Everyone followed Judah and his men to the Holy Temple.

A terrible sight met their eyes. The great doors were burnt and blackened. Weeds grew tall in the courtyard. Soldiers had destroyed the Holy Altar. Statues of Greek gods were everywhere. The Jews wept at what they saw. But everyone quickly set to work restoring the temple.

The statues were taken away. Children helped pull weeds. New doors were brought. The Altar was rebuilt. Craftsmen made new dishes, furniture, and a beautiful gold Menorah lamp. Weavers made curtains for the walls.

The Temple was ready to be dedicated again to God. People came from all over Judea. For eight days, they danced, sang, and praised the Lord. Judah Maccabee spoke to them.

"We will celebrate this great event every year at this time," he said. "Hanukkah means dedication. We will call the holiday 'Hanukkah.'"

THE · LEGEND · OF · THE · MENORAH

When the Holy Temple was ready to be dedicated, Judah Maccabee searched for oil to light the Menorah. The soldiers had smashed the jars. Judah found only one jar, with enough oil for only one day. He decided to light the Menorah anyway. Miraculously, the oil kept burning. It lasted for the eight days of celebration, until new oil was made.

Today, eight lights are lit in the Menorah, one for each night of Hanukkah. The celebration begins on the 25th day of the Hebrew month of Kislev, usually in December. Most Menorahs burn candles, but some have wicks to burn oil, as did the Temple Menorah long ago.

A special candle, the *shammas*, is used to light the menorah candles. New candles are lit each night. A new *shammas* is lit each night, too. The *shammas* is lit first, and the Hanukkah candles are lit from it.

On the first night of Hanukkah, put the first candle at the right end of the Menorah, as you face it. On the second night, two candles, three on the third night, and so on. Always light the newest candle first. Then light the others, from left to right. Place the lighted Menorah in a window, so all may see and share the celebration.

THE · LEGEND · OF · THE · *DREIDLE*

It is said that when King Antiochus would not let the Jews worship God, they prayed and studied secretly. Little wooden tops were kept on tables with the Holy Books. When soldiers came into the houses to make sure the King's orders were being followed, everyone pretended to be playing a game with spinning tops.

During the celebration of Hanukkah, children play with a four-sided top called a *dreidle*. There is a different Hebrew letter on each side. The letters stand for the words: "A great miracle happened there." This refers to the victory of the Maccabees over the King's armies.

T H E · D R E I D L E · G A M E

This is a game for two or more people. You will need a *dreidle* and ten or fifteen items—nuts, raisins or dry beans—for each player.

1. Give each player the same number of items.
2. Each player puts one item from his or her pile into a separate pile called the kitty.
3. Decide who will go first, second, and so on.
4. Each player spins the *dreidle* in turn. The letter that comes up shows what to do:

nun: 　נ　 The player does nothing; it is the next person's turn.

gimel: 　ג　 The player takes the whole kitty. Everyone puts one item in for a new kitty before the next player's turn.

heh: 　ה　 The player takes half of the kitty.

shin: 　ש　 The player puts one item from his or her pile into the kitty.

5. When the kitty is empty, or there is only one item left, each player puts one item from his pile into it.
6. The game is over when a player wins the kitty and the other players have nothing left.

You can buy wood or plastic *dreidles.* You can make your own—it's easy to do.

MATERIALS YOU'LL NEED:

cardboard (an empty laundry soap box is fine), ruler, felt-tipped markers, scissors, pointed stick or pencil, about three inches long.

1. With ruler and pencil, mark a square on the cardboard. Each side should measure two inches long. Cut it out.

2. Draw lines as shown.

3. Draw Hebrew letters as shown.

4. Make a hole in the middle with scissors point. Push pencil stick through, to about halfway. Adjust it to make the *dreidle* spin easily.

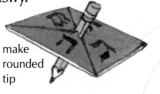

make
rounded
tip

*R*ock of Ages is a traditional song, sung after the Hanukkah candles are lit. It reminds us of the courage of the Maccabees and how, with God's help, they fought for freedom.

ROCK OF AGES (MA-OZ TZUR)

Ma - oz tzur ye - shu - a - ti   le - kha na - eh le sha - be - ah,
Rock of A - ges, let our song   Praise Thy sav - ing___ pow - er;

Tik - kon bet te - fil - la - ti   ve - sham to - dah ne zab - be - ah.   Le
Thou, a - midst the rag - ing foes,   Wast our shel - 'tring___ tow - er.

et ta - khin mat - be - ah   mi - tzar___ ham - nab - be - ah
Fu - rious they as - sailed us,   But Thine arm a - vailed_____ us,

Az eg - mor be - shir miz - mor   ha - nuk - kat ham - miz - be - ah.
And Thy word__ broke their sword   When our own strength failed_ us.

In Hebrew "Maoz Tzur" is a song of praise for the rededication of the Temple.